SUPERMAN
Doesn't Live Here Anymore
III

Listening to the Holy Spirit

Scott McPhillips

Mac on the Attack for Jesus
Honey Creek, Iowa

Copyright © 2011 Scott McPhillips.
Printed and bound in the United States of America.
All rights reserved. No part of this book may be reproduced or transmitted in any form or by any means, electronic or mechanical, including photocopying, recording, or by an information storage and retrieval system—except by a reviewer who may quote brief passages in a review to be printed in a magazine, newspaper, or on the Web—without permission in writing from the publisher. For information, please contact:
Mac on the Attack for Jesus
28535 Coldwater Ave, Honey Creek, IA 51542.

Although the author and publisher have made every effort to ensure the accuracy and completeness of information contained in this book, we assume no responsibility for errors, inaccuracies, omissions, or any inconsistency herein. Any slighting of people, places, or organizations is unintentional.

First printing 2011

ISBN 978-0-9662205-2-0
LCCN 2011926249

ATTENTION CORPORATIONS, UNIVERSITIES, COLLEGES, AND PROFESSIONAL ORGANIZATIONS: Quantity discounts are available on bulk purchases of this book for educational, gift purposes, or as premiums for increasing magazine subscriptions or renewals. Special books or book excerpts can also be created to fit specific needs.
For information, please contact Mac on the Attack for Jesus
28535 Coldwater Ave, Honey Creek, IA 51542.

Web site: hey-scott.com

The Inspiration of Growth:
A COMMENT FROM DAVID HUFFORD

ONCE IN A WHILE A special person comes along who inspires us, not so much by a specific achievement, but by how far they've come. Still more, when a person has been "on the top" sometime in the past and then has fallen, picked himself up, and starts all over again, it is a spiritual thing. When it is very clear that the reason they climbed out and up is because of God and because of faith in God, then we know we are onto something that truly is special.

For me, that special person is Scott McPhillips, whom I have known from a moment in time when he was starting back from his great fall, documented in his first two books. I am honored that he asked me to participate in writing some of those two books, but more so I am inspired to have been part of watching Scott grow from an arrogant athletic has-been to a forceful man of God. It is my watching his steady growth over those past sixteen years that inspires me. Scott has grown into a missionary with a mission, a kinder, more gentle man, a married man (something that is a tremendous blessing for Scott and something I feared would never happen), and—blessing of blessings—Scott is now a father.

I have said in other contexts, "Miracles are sequences." Miracles are not solely some giant parting of the sea; they are a chain of linked events that mark the turning of the soul of one or many to God. And there is no mistake that it is God who put the chain together. The events of Scott's life over the past decade and a half have been just such a chain. And I have been blessed because I not only got to observe it, but also got to be part of it. Scott asked me to write a chapter in his first book and this book and to help him write the second. I have been busy and honored to do so. But this is more than a man's story. It is the text of a miracle because these books are the comment on it.

This comment documents the miracle of human growth to God. And the miracle is the sequence.

PROLOGUE

ALTHOUGH THE BIBLE STATES THAT everyone is created in God's own image, the reality is that we are all but dull reflections, as in a mirror. As we grow and mature (some cases later than others), environmental factors tussle with our instincts, emotions, and spirits to manifest a unique combination we call individuality. No one is perfect; we leave the perfection stuff to God. But I look forward to the day when I will be perfected, that day when God calls me home to live forever with Him in paradise.

The challenge of our lives, of course, is to endeavor each and every waking day to grow ever closer to that perfect One. We sometimes falter and fail; often, we simply run away and hide. Yet God's timetable is not our own. Patience is His superior game because He is unwavering and unchanging in His faithfulness and love for each one of us. Time has little relevance to Him, whether our lives encompass the pages of yesterday, today, or tomorrow. God is, after all, life itself. I would also assert that my life, in particular, despite the grammatical errors in my life's wording, is written in big, bold print.

SCOTT McPHILLIPS: SUPERMAN, SUPER SURVIVOR!

Scott

My Son, Scott

THE FIRST IMPRESSION I GOT from my son was one of impatience. The day he was born, I had been helping my father pick up loose ears of corn around the elevator that had dropped out of the wagon on its way to the corn crib. My mother had supper waiting for us, and we ate a wonderful meal. Afterward, as I was cleaning the dishes at around 8:45 P.M., I felt that first twinge. A short ten minutes later, I felt a second hard twinge, and I half-jokingly said to my mother, "You might be a grandma tonight." Shortly after 9:00 P.M. a third shudder went through me, and my mother immediately went into the living room and woke my husband, who was taking a nap.

"You'd better get into town. I'll keep Steve tonight." (Scott's older brother, Steve, was a toddler.) We left for the hospital, a 15-mile drive, at about 9:15, in the middle of our first measurable snowfall of the season on November 9th. The roads were dark and terribly icy, like a thin layer of glass had been laid over the pavement. Despite the fact that we had just purchased new tires for the car, any speed above 30 mph became an unwelcome and uncontrollable adventure.

Scott's impatience arose to a higher level as soon as we left our driveway, bound for the hospital. Temporary lapses in pain and contractions decreased to just around one minute; Scott had decided to be born, and to be born now! By the time we got to the hospital, the delivery staff was waiting at the door with a wheelchair. They took me straight into a processing room and cut my slacks from my legs (tight buttons were, unfortunately, in high style back then).

A medical staff member exclaimed, "Oh my gosh, this baby's coming!"

They took me immediately into a delivery room, with the rest of my clothes still on and intact. They put my feet up, summoned a resident physician from the Emergency Room, and Scott was suddenly here. Very suddenly here! I felt so sorry for the physician; he had just gotten out of training in baby delivery and had decided from his training he never wanted to see another birth. He was sweating so much; I asked the nurses to wipe his brow so he could see what he was doing. One of the nurses almost chuckled and said, "This isn't the movies; if he wants to see, he can wipe it off with his arm."

By the time my husband got me officially admitted, he was already a father. Scott was born at 9:50 P.M. Impatient.

Today in some ways, not much has changed. He still has an impatient side to him; when he really wants something, he wants it now!

At one point during Scott's rehabilitation after his accident, one of the medical staff advised me, "If Scott was headstrong before his accident, he will be even more so now; if he was manipulative before, it will increase. And if he thought he was a 'ladies' man' before, watch out now. Mom, you haven't got a chance!"

So, was Scott headstrong, manipulative, and a charmer in his youth? When Scott was a baby, he had quite a lusty cry. He made sure somebody responded. Scott began walking at about nine months and was fully potty trained within a year from that point. Funny, but as I recall, after his accident it took Scott about the same amount of time to re-learn those things.

Scott was always climbing, getting into some sort of mischief, commonly defiant; if I spanked him, he would laugh at me. I used to nearly squash him, holding my legs over his, my arms holding him down, asking him if he was ready to talk about "right and wrong" now. After twenty minutes or more of wrestling with him, he would finally relent and say okay. His flailing during that time often left me bruised.

Going to church must have been absolutely entertaining for the church congregation. One second of not holding him securely in my lap and he would be under the pews and headed for the front of the church, unless somebody would capture him on his way.

At four years of age, he began playing chess. One day I remember hearing a terrible noise, and upon entering our living room I discovered my husband had thrown all of the chess pieces across the room. When I asked what happened, he responded, "How would you like it if a four-year-old had just beaten you in chess?"

In kindergarten, Scott's teacher told me she used him to get the kids to play together. If a child was being left out, she would ask Scott to go and get him or her. She knew that if Scott accepted a child into the circle, then everybody would.

I'll never forget the school picnic when Scott was in the second grade. Beebeetown was a smaller school in the area, and after the school year had ended all the parents and children would get together for a large picnic. After eating, the kids all headed off for an energetic relay race. The teachers chose two "volunteers" to go out onto the playground, and the kids were divided into two groups and would race out to a mother, run around her, and run back. Scott's team's mother was a very large woman.

Scott, a high competitor even back then, started yelling at the top of his lungs, "No fair! No fair! She's too big to run around!"

Needless to say, I was very embarrassed. I thought all the other parents were going to faint from laughter, but nobody had the courage to tell Scott why we were all laughing.

When Scott was four years old, his older brother raced a three-wheeled all-terrain vehicle in figure-eight races. After the races were over, Scott would go out and ride on the track by himself. One day he decided to imitate the racers, and in the intersection of the figure eight he flipped the three-wheeler over onto himself. Everyone went running to him, thinking he was really injured, but as we were running, he crawled out from underneath, flipped the three-wheeler over (cussing worse than many adults I've heard), started it up, and took off flying down the track. Always the daredevil. When we talked about the words he was using when he emerged from under the three-wheeler, he said, "That's what everybody says when something's wrong."

Scott has always been quick with his hands. One day he came running into the house with a ground squirrel on one of my kitchen knives, dripping blood all over the kitchen as he ran. He was grinning from ear to ear, having not considered the trouble he was in for having the knife in his possession. Scott has always lived a life of full throttle and wild abandon, which I think is one of the main reasons he recovered to the degree that he has since his accident. On the other hand, it is these same traits that probably caused his accident in the first place.

Scott was always competitive and couldn't stand to lose. At age seven he started playing peewee baseball. It was two years before he was old enough to play in tournaments. He played shortstop. His first experience at pitching was in district tournaments. Grandpa went out to the barnyard with him and caught his pitches. Beebeetown ended up losing 1-0. I was very proud of his effort, but of course, Scott was not happy—they should have won.

As Scott went through high school, I was very proud of his athletic achievements but also of his scholastic "honor roll" grades. He only brought books home "to look good" but had the ability to ace classes without studying. His accounting instructor told us one day, "I knew Scott was copying his homework every day. I would compare his paper to the others and by errors determine who he had copied from that day. But, at test time he never cheated and aced it on his own."

The night of his accident I was walking home from Mom and Dad's place—.3 mile. It was a beautiful fall night, but I could feel something was wrong—Mother's Instinct? Little did I know it was the same time frame that "the accident" had happened.

The uneasiness continued until I went to bed. Ironic as it may seem—this was about the same time help arrived for Scott. When the phone rang after midnight, the caller was a man I went to school and church with. He said, "Scott has been in a terrible accident and is being life-flighted to St. Joseph Hospital. I suggest you get there right away."

Never, as a parent, will you ever feel as helpless as seeing all the doctors and nurses working on your son, trying to save his life, and there's nothing you can do. Then the deputy sheriff came into the waiting room to get a blood sample for alcohol, and I found out that there were two cars involved and that the other driver had been killed—not knowing who at the time. The thoughts that go through your head—"Please, God, please not my son's fault! What have I done wrong in life? What? What? What? Please God—be with the other driver and his family!"

I myself, at that time, had not been as close to God as I should have been. There's nothing like a tragedy to bring your life right with God. You have nowhere to turn but to God and say, "Your Will be done." I always felt that Scott would be okay, but never realized all the trials and tribulations ahead and the time it would take to recover.

God was always there with me to make decisions and give comfort. At three and one half weeks, when they pulled the respirator, the doctors said they had done two brain waves two days in a row and both showed very little activity and what was there was so sluggish that he would be a vegetable for the rest of his life. When they pulled the tube, if he couldn't breathe, did I want them to do a tracheotomy or let him go in peace?

I had already made up my mind as I watched them. "If God has a purpose for Scott's life, he'll breathe on his own. If not, I'll let his organs help others to live." I'll never know if I could have watched Scott die; God let him breathe on his own.

As the doctors, nurses, therapists, a social worker, and I sat around the table discussing Scott's future, there was a desolate feeling—helplessness—as you heard the doctors say, "There is nothing we can do. You need to look for somewhere else for Scott to go—a nursing home?"

Thank God for one nurse and the social worker. They said later he was too young for a nursing home and gave me some options.

When Rebound came to evaluate him, they saw something in his eyes. Little did I know he would be there for two years and two months—but thank God for all their efforts and hard work.

Scott is known for being the only patient to get kicked out of Rebound. He had signed many agreements to be "Appropriate." Wanting to come home, and never being a "Quitter," to get kicked out would be okay.

One of the first talks Scott and I did together was for a Neuro Connection meeting. I can still remember him going up to the doctor and saying in his very slurred speech, "Hi, I'm Scott. I'm the one you said there was no hope for."

He said, "Yes, I know who you are."

Seeing Scott go back to college—letting go in order to let him be on his own—wanting to spare him being made fun of for his speech and walking patterns—was all very hard. Watching him walk across the stage to receive his diploma in 1994 still brings tears to my eyes. Now, to think back to all the people God had him touch while he was there. Mom—let go—let God.

During our many travels across the United States, how often we took a wrong road only to find someone I believe God wanted Scott to talk to. How we were directed to a different diner than the one we were going to, to meet someone who came to God. How we met a minister from California in the Bahamas who invited us to talk at his Church. While in Ceritas, California, we also were led to a minister who had us speak at the Crystal Cathedral. If you let God direct your life—it's an awesome adventure. Let go—let God!

Life has now come full circle. Another phone call. "Mom, can you come to the hospital right away? Debbie's having the baby." I work for a transportation company and was sitting less than a block away at the time. I looked at Creighton Hospital and started crying. Almost twenty-one years ago, right there, when it was called St. Joseph Hospital, where they felt he would be a vegetable for the rest of his life—he was becoming a daddy. Thank you, God!

Reflection—Superman Is in the Building

I WALK THROUGH HALLS OF high school with the confident swagger of a starting tailback. Because I *am* the starting tailback—and linebacker—and punt returner. There is a constant buzz of activity about me, the kind that surrounds people of fame and accomplishment. I am one of the beautiful people, the ones average students try so hard to emulate. The guys give me high fives as they pass; the girls smile, swoon, and swarm. Life is good, and I am good at life.

A super-athlete, I earned all-state honors in football, basketball, and baseball. I wrote the book on high school fame and fortune. Blessed with an arm that could fire off a 94 mph fastball, I was untouchable on the pitching mound. By the end of high school, the Seattle Mariners had come knocking, and I considered heading into Major League Baseball. In the end, though, I went with my first love, football, and received a college scholarship to play for Simpson College in Indianola, Iowa. It was a small college located close to my hometown of Honey Creek, Iowa. A Division III school, it offered solid academics but still retained some of the small-town Iowa charm. And, of course, for me, that meant, just as in high school, being an overgrown shark in a very small pond. Just what I liked.

I was accustomed to all the accolades and perks that go along with the super-athlete status in high school. By the fifth game of my freshman football season at Simpson, I was already the starting free safety. I was living high and large, which manifested itself in an appetite for alcohol, drugs, and girls. Although I had several steady girl friends (often at the same time), in general I simply had any girl I wanted.

DISCUSSION

- *Do you know people like the young Scott McPhillips?*
- *What makes them so influential and powerful?*
- *Is their power of their own making?*
- *Where is God in their lives?*

The Final Warning in 1987

HAVE YOU EVER NOTICED SOME people seem to have the ability to dive into manure and then come up smelling like roses? My wife, Debbie, says this of me. I appear to be one of those people. On the other hand, I am a firm believer that life is what you make of it. And I have a message for you: God has a plan that includes you. In fact, you are the central part of His plan. You need only to discover Him and embrace Him. He will show you the rest. I'll tell you my story, and perhaps you will understand what I mean.

Looking back, of course, I am quite convinced that God really wanted to get my attention; I was simply in no frame of mind to seek Him. If I had, oh, how differently my life's path would have gone! The most obvious warning that my life was on a bad course came during my freshman year of college at Simpson. On a Wednesday night in October of 1987 (interestingly, almost two years to the day before my real story began), I was with a friend, headed west on Interstate 80 in Iowa. We were returning to Indianola after a night of partying of the worst kind in Des Moines. We were both high on alcohol and drugs; my friend was driving the black sports car I had borrowed from my mother. I was passed out in the passenger seat. Only God knows for certain what happened; what is definite is that my friend lost control of the car and it hit a guardrail. I was thrown to my left as my friend was propelled backward. My head slammed against the steering wheel, splitting my skull from my temple, down the right side of my face. As I was being thrown, my left arm caught against the gear shifter and was snapped like a twig.

Seeing the flashing lights of highway patrol cars coming our way and with alcohol in the car, I bailed out, comically yelling at my friend, "I'll see you in the morning, buddy!" I remember escaping from the scene (witnesses said I ran directly across the interstate), jumping a barbed wire fence, and running down a hill and along some railroad tracks before falling on some cinders. One vivid memory that remains today is the sight of the bone grotesquely protruding from my left forearm. Somewhere along the tracks I lost consciousness. Had it not been for my friend, I'm not certain I would have been found, but as the authorities were talking to him, he told them I had run from the scene and was "out there somewhere."

The police helicopter spotted the sheen from the light blue jacket I was wearing. As the rescue squad was carrying me up the hill, I asked them if they had a blanket. Thinking I was cold and going into shock, they were quite concerned. They asked if I was cold. I said, "No," but since they had told me I would be taken in by life-flight, my mind thought of *M*A*S*H* and being taken in on the outside of the helicopter.

They rushed me to a hospital in Des Moines, where surgeons and specialists worked to reconstruct my arm and stitch my face. In total, the gashes to my face required 144 stitches. Although my athletic body healed quickly, I was unable to play football, with a large steel plate in my forearm and a head injury. I tried ineffectively to play baseball, but it quickly became apparent that my athletic career was over.

Without the accolades to which I had become accustomed, my "Superman" self-identity came face-to-face with the forecast of becoming just an average guy, with a steel plate for an arm and a pronounced scar that traced from my temple down my right cheek. My prestige and popularity faded, along with the girls and the friends. I was distant, unattached.

Yet instead of seeking a better alternative, a solution to the questions I'd encountered, I continued along my insane path toward disaster. My grades were atrocious from my lack of academic interest. I soon dropped out of college and returned home, sinking into alcohol and going deeper into the drug trade. I thought it was exciting, and living on this reckless edge was the kind of feeling I missed when the ball had been handed to me in the fourth quarter of a big game. It was a rush, and I reveled in it.

DISCUSSION

- *Can you think of a time when God was trying to get your attention?*
- *How did He do it?*
- *How did you respond?*
- *Why does God care about you?*

A Day of Change

FINALLY, MY DAY OF PERSONAL reckoning had come: October 10, 1989. It would not only be my turning point, but would also forever change the lives of many others through my bad choices, impaired judgment, and ultimate tragedy. Scott Krumwiede, superman and party-boy, was about to meet his obvious fate. If he lived, he might wish he had not. If he died—frankly, the world would not miss him much.

I'd been in town, slurping my way through another evening. I called it quits after about a dozen shots and beers and then, think what you may, I stumbled to my car for the drive home. A friend was entering the bar as I was leaving. "Hey, buddy, how about one more?" We went back in together and threw down one last "drink for the road."

I have lamented many times since that night that I wish I would have died, preferably on the barstool where I had been slamming the alcohol. But God was going to use the circumstances of my fate to His glory. If I had only known; it's easy to say. But I go forward day –by day as is my only choice, with God as my strength, my partner, and my friend.

DISCUSSION

- *Was God involved in Scott's decision process?*
- *Why didn't God intervene in the circumstances that night?*
- *If God is so good, why does He let bad things like this happen?*
- *Did Scott deserve his fate?*

Tom

A LUIS PALAU EVENT IS a Christian invitational festival, drawing thousands of people hungry for a message of hope and promise. The Palau event scheduled in Omaha during July of 2007 was to be no exception. The Second Mile Riders, an Omaha chapter of the Christian Motorcyclists Association, are regularly called to serve in crowd security positions for such events, and, as a member of SMR at the time, I readily volunteered to work the weekend.

I was assigned to work the stage. Basically, my job was to ensure no unauthorized person was allowed to approach the stage and to take appropriate action if anyone was "too enthusiastic" in their intentions to interact with the facilitators, technicians, band members, speakers, and, of course, Luis Palau.

The weekend weather was extremely hot even by Omaha standards for July, which regularly sees temperatures in the 90s during this time of year. By Sunday afternoon, the final day of the festival, nearly 100,000 people had participated in the event throughout the weekend. Temperatures approached triple digits and were easily ten degrees over that among the mass of people crowding the stage. People were fainting, and heat issues were apparent, but the serving volunteers of the Second Mile Riders were there in force, bringing water and comfort to anyone showing signs of overheating.

The day before, on Saturday afternoon, I had been walking among the crowd with several bottles of water (and keeping a careful eye on the stage). As I slowly made my way through the crowd, the man directly in front of me caught my eye. He walked with an upright and stiff gait, as if he were walking with a pole strapped from his neck to his ankle. He was about my height at a little over 6 feet although as he walked he had to lean forward. His hair was cut to about a quarter of an inch all around, and he was wearing a white sleeveless T-shirt and cut-off jean shorts.

I assumed he was mentally challenged, but he did not appear dangerous. He was simply another festival attendee enjoying an afternoon of music and hope. He walked stiff-legged with a large metal brace on one knee, along the sidewalk about three yards in front of me.

The sidewalk sloped downward just a little, and the man did not see the slope. When his measured stagger encountered the slope, his stiffened body could not compensate and, suddenly, down he went, head first onto the concrete. He didn't even raise his hands to brace his fall and, instead, took the full impact on his shoulders and head.

Instantly, there was a crowd surrounding him with help, water, and assistance. My instinct was to do the same, but, in the interest of my primary purpose of security, I held back and observed the helpful crowd before getting involved. As they helped him up, with a slight cut to his forehead, I could see why he hadn't raised his hands to protect his fall. Both hands were shriveled like those of a victim of a stroke, and his arms were bent and severely restricted in their range of motion. He was laughing. Laughing out loud. People dabbed at the cut with tissues; they offered water; they laughed along with him. I moved on.

So here it was, Sunday afternoon, and I was beginning to look forward to the final address from Luis Palau that evening and the closing of a long, crowded, and hot weekend. Suddenly, I received a rather heightened call from Susan, another security volunteer on the opposite side of the stage.

"Tom, I need you here fast. This guy is trying to get up on stage. He's scary, and he's saying scary things. Get here," she said.

"Is Rich with you?" I inquired. Rich is Susan's husband and had just retired from a career in the United States Air Force. I was confident that Rich would be able to handle any sort of crisis situation with logic and quick decisions.

"Yes, he's here. But this guy is different. We don't know what to do," she said.

Brief though the conversation was, by the time it was over I had Susan in sight. There she was, face-to-face with the same guy I had witnessed fall to the sidewalk the day before. But this time he was not smiling or laughing. He was yelling. Unintelligible words were spraying from his mouth as his tongue was certainly no match for the enthusiasm of his brain.

I forcibly wedged myself between them, getting uncomfortably close to the man as I slowly and carefully backed him away and all the time talking softly with him in even tones in an effort to settle him down. I smiled a tense, forced smile.

"So what's your name?" I asked.

"I'm Scott McPhillips!" he yelled with force.

"Well hey, Scott, I'm Tom. What's your story?"

"I'm here to see Luis. I want to talk to him."

"Luis is not here. Where were you when he was here signing books and giving autographs for an hour and a half earlier this afternoon? I'm sorry, Scott, but you've missed him. He's back at his hotel."

"I want to see him!" Scott demanded.

"He's not here."

Scott moved to the side slightly, as if going for the stage. I quickly moved to his front and blocked his passage.

"Nobody goes on stage, Scott. Nobody. Look, Luis is gone. Let's not let this get out of hand. Why do you need to see Luis, anyway?"

Scott began to settle down. He made eye contact. His voice lowered, and his posture softened. I don't know if it was my presence, the fact that somebody was finally listening to him, or the Omaha police standing a few feet behind me, ready to take Mr. McPhillips to jail.

Over the next twenty minutes or so, I listened to Scott's impassioned plea to see Luis Palau. He felt that Luis would benefit from hearing his story, and he knew if Luis listened to him that both lives would be changed. Looking back at it, Scott was actually and very probably correct. As our conversation progressed, I came to know that this guy was not, as I had assumed the day before, mentally impaired in any way. Although his body was contorted, his head displayed obvious scars from some earlier tragedy, and his speech was very slurred, I could tell by his sentence patterns that he was lucid.

And a curious thing—every few minutes he would seem to recognize somebody in the crowd and would yell at them, make a gesture with his shriveled arm, and get a happy and enthusiastic response. People actually seemed to know Scott McPhillips.

Scott was passionately driven to see Luis Palau. But I had been truthful; Luis had, indeed, returned to his hotel. I worked with Scott, always having the police directly behind me, for what seemed like an hour before finally working a "deal" with him.

"Here's the deal, Scott. You need to leave this event. Right now. I am going to escort you off the property, and you are not to return. If you do, you will be arrested for trespassing. In return, I'm going to give you my card. You call me on Monday, and I will buy you lunch. I will listen to your story. That's my final offer."

I thrust my business card to him as an offer to seal the agreement. If he had not taken my card, I am sure the police would have moved in. But, to everyone's surprise, he accepted my card. We shook hands. The mood lightened. And I began the process of escorting Scott McPhillips through the crowd and off the property.

Amazingly, a walk that should have taken five minutes took every bit of forty-five. Not because of Scott's uncoordinated stagger, but because people kept coming up to him and shaking his hand, hugging him, or just wanting to talk to him. Everybody seemed to know this guy! I felt like I was escorting a rock star. *Who was Scott McPhillips?*

One Monday Morning

TRUTHFULLY, THE LAST THING I expected was that Scott would actually call me. But on Monday morning a call came to my office at the local nonprofit where I was employed. I quickly identified the caller's voice as the slurred, tongue-tied pattern of Scott McPhillips.

"I want to meet with you. You said you would listen to my story," Scott said.

"Yes, and I will. I'll buy you lunch. Where should we meet?' I asked.

"Meet at the diner in Crescent. Noon."

"Okay, Scott, I'll see you at noon."

I walked into Henry's Diner in Crescent at the appointed time, and there sat Scott in his white muscle shirt and cutoffs, talking trash with the local patrons. He sipped water through a straw, and it wasn't uncommon to see half of what he sucked dribble from his chin down onto his shirt.

Honestly, I was thinking that this was the price I was to pay for getting Scott to leave the Luis Palau event without incident. I'll listen. I'll display interest. I'll buy his lunch, shake his hand, and leave. And that will be the end of it.

God, however, had other plans. What I assumed to be simply fulfilling an obligation was to become an ongoing relationship with a walking miracle of a man. It was to result in a deepening of my faith in a loving and healing Christ, and it was to be an astounding testimony to me of how God can work in the life of anyone, including Scott McPhillips. Including me. Including you.

Scott began to tell me the story of his athletic high school success, of his achievements, his high school records in football, basketball, and baseball. Some of the records remain intact even today, over twenty years later. I knew the type of person he was in high school; we all know of these people—the untouchable athletes who seem to have everything come so easily, the fame, the friends, the women, the good times. I had been a decent athlete myself in high school but never tried out for an organized sport. As such, I had felt out of place, excluded from high school, an outcast. But now as I listened to Scott, I was confronted with my lingering feelings of resentment for people like Scott, contrasted with the Scott of today, who simply needs somebody to listen to his story. In Scott, I have the choice to resent or forgive; there is no middle ground.

On October 10, 1989, Scott had left the bar after his evening of beer and faded glory, bound for his home nestled in the Loess Hills, approximately twenty miles away. His car weaved and wandered as by now the night's alcohol had taken full control of his mind and body. Some people, when driving drunk, tend to slow down and hug the curb, seeming to feel unsure of their situation and longing to reach their destination. With other drunks, like Scott, the more they drink, the more bulletproof they feel. These drivers put the pedal to the metal, flop a wrist over the top of the steering wheel, and just assume the world will watch out for them and their speeding vehicle. It didn't.

Cresting a hill on a gravel road that night, Scott's life of fated fortune ran out. He hit the oncoming car head-on at a very high rate of speed. The driver of the other car, the best friend of Scott's older brother, was killed instantly as his neck was snapped from the force created by steel and speed. It was over two hours before an approaching vehicle discovered the accident and alerted the authorities. Everybody assumed both drivers had died. But Scott remained very faintly alive.

The rescue squad at the scene of the accident discovered the mangled and motionless body of Scott crumpled inside the wreckage of metal and glass. In the whirling, chaotic moment there the emergency personnel checked on the driver of the other vehicle. Finding that the other driver had died, they started working on Scott. Using the jaws of life to free him, thinking that he was free, they started to extricate him but found that his foot was encased in metal. Time was of the essence; cut off his foot to save his life or leave him intact for his family? The firemen at that time felt that despite his faint but resilient heartbeat, Scott would soon be leaving this world anyway. Sometimes in these situations the reasoning is strange and faulty, but the implications of that decision were monumental.

And so they took an additional half an hour to remove Scott from the car, carefully cutting around his extremities and slowly removing his body for transport to the hospital. Yet even with the extra time, Scott's heart kept going.

From the time of removing Scott from the car, it was another half an hour before they had him to the hospital. Altogether, considering the lag time before being discovered, waiting, decision making, cutting him from the car, stabilizing him, and carefully loading him into the life-flight, it was over four hours before Scott arrived for treatment. Throughout all this time, Scott's heart refused to stop.

Scott fell into a coma, and during the first several days most were mentally preparing for the long, slow arrival of a quiet death. Scott missed Halloween and his twenty-first birthday; he was in a coma. He missed the Thanksgiving meal, the entire Christmas season. The coma continued throughout the winter. Scott's body shriveled, his hands curling, his arms and legs drawing up into a fetal position.

Spring of 1990 came forth with the smells and colors of the flowers in the Midwest, the last of a winter snow blanket melted away, yet Scott remained in his coma. It was graduation time, and kids were preparing for the transition to college. Another baseball season rolled around, but Scott would not be participating. Coma. Easter, Memorial Day, the Fourth of July. Scott hovered in his fetal prison between life and death.

Then, in late July of 1990, Scott's body began to show the first signs of a reawakening. His eyes fluttered, muscles twitched. Over the course of several days, Scott slowly became aware of the world around him—a new world where he was confined to a cocoon and unable to break out. Welcome to your body, your new reality, Scott.

Nine months in a coma takes its toll. Far beyond not being able to walk or talk, it was as if his brain had been a computer where, although the hard drive had remained intact, every application had been erased. Personality, social skills, communication even on the most basic levels—absolutely everything had to be relearned. Was he left-handed or right? To this day, Scott will tell you that he continues to rehabilitate in body, mind, and soul.

Scott spent the initial twenty-six days after his accident in the Intensive Care Unit of St. Joseph Hospital and one month more in a private room. This was followed by two months of rehabilitation at Immanuel Hospital in Omaha and then over two years in the Rebound program of Independence Regional Hospital in Independence, Missouri. Scott came home two and a half years later to the day—April 10, 1992. Fueled by his tenacious internal drive to walk, talk, think, and feel again, he's had over six thousand hours of therapy, followed by an additional ten thousand hours on his own. It was the most difficult thing he has ever done, but his hunger to return to a life of "normalcy" was unbounded.

The rehab hospital had its moments and hours of boredom, particularly with a body that needed assistance to do, well, anything. The chaplain would come by weekly and read to Scott from the Bible, something that Scott dreaded. But there was nothing he could do about it. And during one preordained visit by the chaplain, something inside Scott told him to pay attention. Scott accepted the call of Christ in his life on February 19, 1991, at 12:35 P.M.

God took a hard-living, super-hero-turned-druggy-and-drunk, confined to a hospital bed and imprisoned in a body that could no longer cooperate, and made him an evangelist for Christ. God has plans for everybody, and on this day Scott was chosen to play a part. From that time on, Scott's new drive to rehabilitate his wracked and broken body was motivated by a call to testify about the saving grace of God. And God was painting a future for Scott that would take him all over the world.

So here I sat at Henry's Diner in Crescent, Iowa, as Scott unraveled his story before me. I was speechless; I'd never heard anything like it before. There is no story like the story of Scott McPhillips. Miracle—simply a miracle. That's all I kept thinking; it's all I could say for the rest of the day. This guy is a walking, talking, living, breathing miracle. I've been working with Scott, advising him regarding his life and business affairs since that day at the diner.

DISCUSSION

- *Why did Tom get involved with Scott's story?*
- *How is the Scott of today like the Scott of yesterday?*
- *Would you have taken the extra step and listened to Scott?*
- *Do you know somebody like Tom?*

Small Voices

WITH THE CLARITY OF RETROSPECTION, I see now that God often uses the circumstances of my own haughty tendencies to try to get my full attention. It seems to manifest itself sometimes in the little things. The recollections of my youth, of my growing up, are faded now—no, more accurately, wiped absolutely clean in one broad stroke. I remember only a few sketchy details of life before my accident, and that which I do remember I have embellished to the point that I can't really differentiate between fact and fiction. And although October 10, 1989, was the turning point in my life's story, even within the last few years I admit that at times I have struggled to heed the guidance of the Holy Spirit.

A case in point happened during a cruise to Mexico in May of 2006; I fell back to some old habits and addictions. Hitting the gambling tables, it took me no time at all to lose $600. It doesn't seem like a lot of money when I look back on it now, but at the time it was money I could not afford to lose. I remember hearing that "still, small voice" of the Holy Spirit telling me that there were better choices to be made; gambling was not a demonstration of wisdom. Yet in the end, at least that night, I chose not to heed the voice. I had to try my own way and, consistent with my pattern, paid a price I could ill afford.

To emphasize and exacerbate the problem that particular night, I had gotten drunk while I was gambling (yes, my demons were surely winning that night). Later, after I had lost the money and left the gambling table in a depressed and drunken stupor, I fell on my previously broken shoulder. Since my accident, I have fallen a lot. I tried to count how many times I have landed on my face and shoulders; I stopped counting at 150. To date, I've broken my left collarbone five times and my right one four. But on this night I fell on my right shoulder, which had been frozen because of the traumatic injury it had sustained since my accident. What should have sent me rocketing in pain in a strange way proved Romans 8:28 to be good advice to live by: "And we know that in all things God works for the good of those who love Him, who have been called according to his purpose." At any rate, something in my shoulder popped or suddenly gave way from the impact of the fall, and this joint that had constantly throbbed all these years immediately settled down and stopped hurting to such a debilitating degree. Yes, even when we screw up, God still loves us, and sometimes finds a way to let us know. Do I recommend my stupidity for other people? Not hardly. Was my drunken gambling a good pattern of circumstantial choice? No. It demonstrates the magnificence and patience of a loving God.

People make excuses for their poor choices every day, just as I have. And as relatives, friends, and coaches used to try to help me discover the straighter path, in the end it was I, "Superman," who wandered off. Perhaps in a way, my own wayward path of high price gives me license now to recommend a different course for others. I can tell people what I think they need to do to work their way out of a bad situation, and they may even agree with me. "I know, I know, I know," they say. It may be a cliché, but I tell them straight and bluntly—then just do it, baby. Do it the right way. Live life in "righteousness," and God will bless you for it. And when you mess up and get out of line (we all do), don't run deeper into the darkness but instead run to Jesus. God is so great He will turn it out for our good! Great is His name. Greatly to be praised.

DISCUSSION

- *Why does God seem sometimes to pull back from involvement in your life?*
- *Have you had times when you did not heed the Holy Spirit's guiding advice?*
- *Is there a correlation between how much time you spend with God and your ability to recognize His voice?*
- *How can you draw nearer to God on a consistent basis?*

Respecting the Limitations

WHEN I PUSH MY BODY too hard, calamity results. My body, after all, is not like that of the average guy on the street. My body has been crushed and is still hampered by injury, broken and challenged by my accident. On August 1, 2006, I pushed myself too hard at the Old Market in downtown Omaha. Sometimes I feel such a spiritual burden for people, and I mistakenly interpret this as God's personal call to me to save the world. Of course, it's not me that does any "saving" at all. That has already been done by Jesus Christ. But I assertively "street-witnessed" on the crowded and confined streets of the Old Market, approaching anybody when the opportunity presented itself. It was very hot, and I was not paying any attention to my fragile body.

By the time I got home, I'd become aware that I was hurting badly and was having a very difficult time walking and keeping my balance. As I entered my bathroom, my body finally gave out; I lost my balance and fell into the bathtub. I never lost consciousness, but ouch! When I fall, bad things can happen because I am unable to react as people instinctively do, by putting their hands out. My hands and fingers will no longer extend, so when I fall I tend to land on my shoulders, collarbone, and head! Praise God I didn't break anything. God was trying to remind me once again that I was not Superman. I know I'm not, but the old Scott, the one that never quits and pushes everything to its ultimate, still lives in me and routinely chides me into going beyond my own limitations.

I stretch my wrecked and shattered body every morning. I will do whatever is necessary to stretch my body out to make it feel like it should, a lingering discipline from two years in a rehabilitation hospital. In a way, I believe my body is a lot like many peoples' souls; we often abuse them and try to make them conform to a world for which they are not designed. Just as with my scarred body, the best thing to do is not to look in the mirror and not be captivated by hindsight. It might scare you.

DISCUSSION

- *How do you react when you have tried to do too much?*
- *What does God say about pacing yourself?*
- *Has God ever taken time to rest?*

Hard Times

TODAY IS A DIFFICULT DAY. Sometimes I have a lot of problems reading my own writing. I am constantly reminded through my uncooperative motor skills of the choices I made many years ago that have impacted my day-to-day life. I face some form of this every day. My hands have been injured beyond complete repair (they shake involuntarily), and so today I laboriously read the journal writing that looks like it came from a four-year old. Progress is slow, but even my decrepit hands are gradually getting better over time—never good and never reliant, but at least better. I'll never forget the day in physical rehabilitation when the therapists tried to open my hands and fingers, which had curled during the many comatose months following the accident. It was the worst pain of my life, and just one of many times when I wish I had died.

Rehabilitation of a body, and of a spirit, takes a long time, and in most cases takes place not without further brokenness and scarring. Healing does not occur according to our timeline, but only in accordance with God's perfect time. My responsibility is to do the things that promote healing. In the case of my body, I continue to walk, to work, simply to keep active with what remains. With regard to my spirit, I turn it over to a faithful and merciful God, who helps me to fight Satan's battle against me each day. I spend hours in prayer, study the Word of God unceasingly, and tell of God's healing daily. My spirit is the much greater prize, but Jesus has already paid the price for my eternity, a hope which I cherish as I look toward my everlasting future.

Satan will lie to you every step of the way. He wants to mislead, cheat, and destroy you. He only wants to ruin you. God gave you life and that more abundantly. I was living the Devil's lie in my life until I was twenty-one. I wrecked several cars, killed someone. I am sometimes asked if I feel remorseful. Yes, but I cannot change the past. I deal with the problems and the circumstance no matter what and just try day –by day to get on down the road. I've certainly learned the hard way that although God is in control of everything, there are still consequences to our actions.

On September 22, 2006, I went to a football game at my old high school (Tri- Center). It really hurt me, after the winning tradition we built, to see them get trounced 49-7. In my day we had quite a run of state qualifiers, two state runners-up and one state championship. I am very proud of my high school, junior high, and elementary school. Tri-Center is a fine school with good teachers, good parents, and a good community. I contrast my memories of the life I used to live with the one I live now. Life is indeed a journey; the challenge is to enjoy the *entire* ride.

If I'm not actively doing something, I feel worthless, and Satan lies to me. That trite old saying has a lot of truth in it: An idle mind is the Devil's playground. I know I need to rest often, but I battle my own feelings that nothing good can come of laziness. I am always trying to balance my need for rest and the temptation of laziness. My wife sometimes calls me "lazy boy." I can be lazy on one day and then push myself beyond my physical and mental limits the next. I just try to genuinely rest when I rest, play hard when I play, and minister effectively when I minister. Does God love me? Yes. Does God love you? Yes. We are His workmanship.

I met a woman named Eileen at the Open Door Mission in Omaha, Nebraska, where I was speaking one day. She got me involved in doing her TV show with her, which resulted in me getting my own TV show. I had my own TV show for eight months. It got really overwhelming, trying to get my guests to do shows. Everyone seemed ever-so-eager to commit to doing a guest spot on the show, but they would often ultimately back out. It frustrated me (and I admit I am easily frustrated). So I ended my show. Some people were very faithful and honored their commitments to the show, and for them I am thankful. But, ultimately, it was best that we closed that chapter in my story.

I recall falling on a freshly waxed floor at the TV studio one day. I was in a lot of pain and remember telling the producer, "Just give me a Darvocet; the show must go on." I had some Darvocet, a painkilling medication, in my car. It's easy to fall into the habit of masking pain with medication; it is a battle I will fight the rest of my life. We did the TV show that night. I went to the doctor the next day and discovered I had broken two ribs. Pain is nothing new to me. In a twisted sort of way, I kind of like it. It reminds me of my old glory days on the football field. My real glory days are different now, praising the Lord Jesus Christ (God). Since my fall at the studio, I have been on Eileen's show, *God in my Corner*, several times with my wife—at a new location in a new studio.

DISCUSSION

- *How would you explain Scott's statement, "Although God is in control, there are still consequences to our actions"?*

- *What is the difference between rest and laziness?*

- *Scott has often masked his physical pain with medication. How do you mask your pain?*

Out of Control

WE ALL LIKE TO FEEL important. I am no different. I would pre-tape a month's worth of TV shows, then fly off around the world somewhere, speak, and distribute books. I did this for eight months. Eventually, I couldn't do it anymore; it was too much for me. We all think we can handle more than we are able to. God will never give anyone more than they can handle. It's easy in our enthusiasm to bite off more than we can chew. We think, "I can handle this or that without God," but, really, we can handle nothing. You can only ultimately prosper in life when you have God in your corner.

At the time of this writing (it was a much-needed blessing), my wife and I went to Henry's Diner in Crescent, Iowa. Henry's remains my favorite local haunt; everyone needs to eat there at least once. We had a prime rib supper, and someone I gave my books to some time ago paid for our meal. It was quite an unexpected gift. Thank you, God, for blessing me.

Here is a challenge I personally want to throw out to every person who reads this book. Do you think you are a good person? If you really want to know the answer, look into a mirror and say, "I love you." If you have problems in your actions or moods, you will look away. Positive people are able to look in the mirror and say, "I love you," because they are upstanding, good people striving to be the best they can be.

I'm getting really tired of spending so many hours out distributing my books. The physical and mental wear and tear is never ending. I go out and bust my butt every day. I can't blame anyone; I choose to do it because I love everyone. At one time I

DISCUSSION

- *How would you define a "good" person?*
- *How does God define a "good" person?*
- *Can you name examples of good people?*
- *Are they perfect people?*
- *Are there any perfect people?*

was averaging about three or four pain pills a day. I needed to take them because my knees hurt. I have gradually cut back on the pain pills, and now I only take one or two per day. I am working to get rid of them completely.

Debbie

I WAS BROUGHT UP IN a Christian home, in the knowledge of the Lord, in Bristol, England. My father is a Christian, and I would go to church with him as a child—and continued going to church as I grew older. I asked the Lord and Savior Jesus Christ into my heart when I was eight years old. But it has only been since about the age of nineteen that I have trusted in Him day by day to guide and counsel me.

My family and I had been coming to the United States on holiday for several years; we went to Florida for the first time in 1994, loved it, and returned yearly for several days of winter sun. We loved to travel, and Florida was our favorite holiday destination. Up until the time I met Scott, I'd been praying for a husband for nineteen years. By this time I was beginning to wonder whether there was someone for me, and I was starting to resign myself to the life of a single woman.

When I met Scott, I was on our yearly holiday (on vacation, as you say in the United States) with my family in Orlando, Florida. It was Tuesday, March 1st, 2005. We had actually planned to arrive a week earlier but were unable to get a flight. Had we done so, I may not have ever met Scott. We arrived in Florida on Sunday, February 27th.

We were staying at Orlando's Vacation Villas at Fantasy World, the same resort where Scott and his mom, Beverly, were also staying. We were only there for that week, as we were leaving to stay in another resort at the end of the week. We were staying in a two-bedroom townhouse, and Scott and his mom were staying in a two-bedroom apartment in a high-rise. These units shared the same pool.

It was Tuesday morning. The weather was hot, sunny, and beautiful. I was sunbathing by the pool, which was part of my normal Florida routine of swimming, sunbathing, tanning (all those tourist things). When I go to the pool, I use the opportunity to pray and meditate on God's Word, and I usually take my Bible with me.

It was just like any other day on holiday, and I was relaxing and had no idea that my world was about to get turned upside down. Suddenly, I heard a scraping sound coming toward me. I opened my eyes and saw a man walking toward me in a labored gait. He looked mentally challenged; the sound I had heard was a metal leg brace he was wearing as it scraped against the concrete pool deck with each of his purposeful steps. I was scared, because in my relatively minimal experience with mentally challenged people, I had found them to be somewhat unpredictable. I thought to myself, "What does he want? Get rid of him quick." He asked me if he could show me his book, but I couldn't fully understand what he was saying at first. He repeated his question as he took a book from his bag and gave it to me.

I could tell straight away that it was about him, and it was his picture on the back. "It's you," I said. He said, "You're pretty bright, aren't you?" I decided to buy his book; I typically respond favorably to charity whenever I am approached. However, I hadn't taken money with me to the pool, so I said, "I'll have to go back to the room to get some money." He asked if he could sit down on my sun bed as I looked through his book, and we started talking. When I saw the picture of his car in the book, I realized my first impression of him had been incorrect. Scott was "normal," whatever that means.

He was wearing what I thought was a cowboy hat, so my first impression of him was that he had been a cowboy. His book, *Superman Doesn't Live Here Anymore*, would tell a different story. Scott was no cowboy; he had been an athlete. I left him sitting on the sun bed while I went to get some money to give him, all the time wondering, who is this man? Is he for real, and can he be trusted?

I returned to the pool and gave him ten dollars for the book. We continued to talk for quite a while, and by the end of our initial conversation, feelings for him had been stirred. Scott had made me feel like I had never felt. He made me feel important and special. At one point in our conversation, as we grew closer by the moment, our intimacy resulted in his leaning toward me with a hug and a kiss. I turned and offered my cheek, but he was very persistent. His persistent lips met mine. It seemed so forward, but, admittedly, I liked it. Something inside me stirred; I was so unaccustomed to feeling the sparks racing through me. When it was time for us to part, he asked me to write to him and stay in touch, so I said I would. The rest of that day I wondered, "Who was that? What just happened? Did that really happen?" My life has not been the same since that day.

Later that week, on Friday afternoon, my dad and I went over to the pool, and Scott and his mom were sitting by the pool. As our conversation became easier and our relationship grew deeper, we talked and prayed together. Scott was not shy about his dream of marriage and settling down. I, on the other hand, was just getting to know him—and, for that matter, myself. I was distracted by his obvious disabilities. Ultimately, Scott and I made arrangements to meet at the pool the next morning, which was also our last day in the resort.

On Saturday morning we met at the pool as arranged and spent a couple of hours together talking and getting to know each other. My dad came over to the pool, and Scott and he talked for a while. Then Scott invited my dad and me up to his apartment to meet his mom. So we went up to the apartment with him and met Beverly, who was very nice, and we had coffee with them.

When it was time for us to part for the last time, we agreed to stay in touch by letter and email, and he invited me to come visit him in Iowa. I assumed it to be a sort of "cursory" invitation, a non-binding idea. We went our separate ways, staying in touch by mail and email.

DISCUSSION

- *How did Debbie get beyond Scott's initial appearance and see the "inside man"?*
- *What is the basis of love?*
- *How does love form?*
- *How does love display itself?*

Seeing Beyond

AS TIME PROGRESSED, WE CONTINUED to grow closer through our email/snail mail contacts. Finally, I visited him in September 2005 and again in April 2006 and then *again* in April 2007. When I first met Scott, all I could see was his disability. But once we had started talking and I found out he is this way because he was in a car accident, I was able to see past his disability and saw something of the man inside the broken body. Through our conversations I had come to really enjoy being around Scott. In fact, when we were not together, he was all I could think about. I genuinely liked him; he was so engaging, so genuine, so disarming, and very funny. At first I thought he was sort of cute, but the longer I have spent with him the more "cute" has grown into "attractive." In retrospect I recognize now that I was quickly coming to love him deeply. Soon my entire self-concept was intertwined with his.

Also, although he is an extrovert and I am an introvert, we are very alike in a lot of ways. We have a lot in common. We were designed for each other before time began. We like a lot of the same music, and we share the same sense of humor. We have a lot of joy together, and we are always laughing. I prayed for someone who is not boring. Scott is the opposite of boring! I got what I prayed for and then some. He is the most confident person I have ever met; he is not afraid of anyone or anything.

In that way he is the opposite of me. I had grown up in a rough neighborhood. Every day it seemed I was threatened. Getting bullied by other kids was not at all uncommon. I'd seen the physical results early in my childhood when my sister experienced such bullying. As a result, I felt unable to stand up for myself. Instead, I became a shy and quite unknown recluse.

It was difficult having a long-distance relationship, and I asked God many times whether I should continue in this relationship, whether it was His will, and I asked Him to end it if it wasn't His will. I also fasted and prayed about it and asked Scott on the phone whether he wanted to end it or not; he didn't even want to entertain the conversation. All along I believed that this was God's will and knew that I had to give him to God if I wanted him to be my husband. On April 19, 2007, Scott proposed to me, saying that he had known for some time that we were headed in this direction. He also said that God had told him that He had hand-picked me for him and told him to propose. Scott is always joking.

Up to that point I hadn't seen him ever this serious, so I thought he was joking when he proposed, and I laughed in response. But Scott wasn't laughing; he was unwavering and resolute. I was certainly not expecting this, though I had been hoping for it. When I realized he was indeed serious, Scott confided to me that God had told him that I was the one. I could see the commitment in his eyes and feel it in his heart. I said, "Yes, I'll marry you."

Scott took me straight to Brodkey's Jewelers in Oakview Mall in Omaha, Nebraska, about thirty-five miles away, to get an engagement ring and the wedding rings. Oakview Mall is a very smart, modern, big mall and seems to be very popular. He chose this jeweler because he was already a customer there and knew the people who work there; he is good friends with them. It was a very special time, picking out the rings, and very exciting for me.

I was so very happy and excited and also a bit scared and overwhelmed. After all, it is a big step to take and should not be entered into lightly. Marriage is for the rest of your life. But I believe if we keep putting God first and trust Him, then everything will turn out just fine.

And now, more than three years since our wedding, this has proved to be true. God is blessing us richly. Our love has grown and continues to grow. This is true for everyone if you want real joy in your life, Jesus number one, others number two, and you number three. We all get them mixed up because we are all human.

I arrived in Iowa on September 7, 2007. I was initially to stay for a week, but we decided we didn't want to be apart anymore. So I stayed and we married on his birthday, November 9, 2007. We make a special effort to go and see my family as often as we are financially able.

When I consider the enormity of the life-changing events I have experienced lately, I am overwhelmed by the impact and the speed with which things have transpired. Meeting Scott. Falling in love. Coming to the U.S.A. Ultimately, marrying Scott and settling here. Now a mother to our beautiful daughter. And, of course, with all of that, I cannot help but remember all I've given up to follow this path. I had put my trust firmly in the Lord; it was the most challenging leap of faith I had ever taken. I began in simplicity, taking one day at a time and enjoying just that day. I resisted looking too far ahead and have found that as I live in this momentary state I enjoy life so much more than I had before.

Yet I love Scott more each and every day. We spend all day every day together, and we still can't get enough of each other. Whenever we are apart, I miss him and can't wait to be with him again. I see how hard he works at distributing his books. He is dripping with sweat in very hot temperatures, and it doesn't phase him. His heart really is in it. Being from England, I am not used to the heat and humidity here, and I can't stay out in the sun like he does. I think it is incredible how he can stay so cheerful, given the challenges he faces every day and how hard he works. I really do admire him and thank him for the brilliant way he takes care of me.

I will never fully know what Scott was like before his car accident, but he tells me he was so off the edge, so out of control. Now I see it displayed in his humor and his charisma. Age and his traumatic experience have refined and tempered him tremendously. I have read the newspaper clippings about him and seen the photographs, and I am glad I fell in love with the new Scott.

God has been working on me, continually molding and shaping me, since I have been living in the United States. My confidence has grown greatly; I am a different person from the one who moved to the U.S.A. just three years ago.

When we went to England in March 2009, the Lord began to encourage me to speak alongside Scott as he spoke to various church groups. Each time I rose to speak, it felt easier than the previous time. The nerves calmed with repetition. (I'd never had the opportunity to speak to a large audience before.) When we returned home to the states, I accompanied Scott and spoke at a middle school, soon followed by a Hispanic church in south Omaha. I simply said a few words about how Scott and I met and how God's plans are often magnificently unexpected. Today, the nagging nervousness before large crowds is almost gone, and I sense God encouraging me to deliver a deeper message of loving and falling in love with a guy like Scott.

DISCUSSION

- *Is love enough for a lifetime relationship?*
- *Can love die?*
- *What role do trust and commitment play in a long-lasting relationship?*

Scott About Debbie

I CANNOT MATCH DEBBIE'S STORY of praying for a spouse for nineteen years, but I had been praying for about five years for a wife. I was not ready for a wife until Debbie came along. Since God tapped me on my broken shoulder and rescued me, I had been living a polarized life between His plan for me and my own high-strung ego. Now, with Debbie at my side and serving as a calming helpmate, I am able to stay more focused on God's mission and put aside my own wants (at least, most of the time).

As my rehabilitation began to bear fruits and my body came back to life along with my mind, I have been able to put my story in print. I needed to find a way to support myself, and writing a book seemed to be a good answer to the dilemma; a second book soon followed the first. I walk the streets of every town and city I encounter, selling those books one by one to put food on the table. I have distributed more than forty thousand books to date, and now with Debbie in my life, we have begun to write a third one together. I'm not getting rich by any accounting, but God's love for me runs deeper than the quest for money, and my love for Him makes distributing the books both an adventure and a blessing.

I believe very strongly in my books; they tell a true story, and I have lived it. I probably give away about as many as I sell. But I am leveraging my experience for God's purpose; His love is worth so much more than money and is far more important to me than riches. My first book is about my sports background and prior life, my accident and recovery, and the long, painful road back. The second book focuses on an experience I had when I met Jesus face-to-face at Heartland of America Park in Omaha, Nebraska, one evening from 8:05 to 8:30 P.M. on September 9, 2004. Jesus told me that "Rabboni is happy, very happy with you. Keep doing what you're doing." So I am. I wrote about it. My books are intended to help people and to give them hope so they won't make the same mistakes I did. They were written for everyone; we all need help.

My first thought when I approached Debbie poolside on that divinely appointed morning was, "This is an *Okay* woman." I fully realized who I was in Christ Jesus, but I still had some uncertainty in my life. I did not have a clear vision of God's plan for my life. But, well, who does? No one, of course, except God himself. Still, I had an immediate impression (perhaps by the prompting of the Holy Spirit that lives within each of us) that Debbie was going to play a very important role in my life.

As our initial conversation progressed to feelings deep within our hearts, feelings we had had for a long time, it lead to a first kiss that I will never forget. The Holy Spirit said, "You just kissed your future wife" (to which I replied, "No way"). I wasn't prepared for the impact of Debbie, and in a way the Holy Spirit made a fool of my stubbornness once again. At any rate, I was intrigued by Debbie. Still caught up in some of my old life and my carnal view of the world at times, I was not looking for a "common" person. I had in mind perhaps a model, an actress, or a rock star—but not a European on holiday! Today, looking back at our immediate connection and subsequent life commitment to each other, I am happier than I have ever been. As we were getting to know each other better, I would silently pray, "If you do want us together, she will need to come over here to America." I continued to feel God's patient leading, and I eventually invited Debbie to come to visit my home in Iowa.

God had a laugh that day by the pool. Debbie ended up buying more than my book. Isn't it funny how we all have our own plans? We think we know best; God just sits back and keeps His hands off and has a laugh. He thinks, "When will they learn?" God has *perfect* plans for all of us. We try and work out our own plans. We fall on our face (in my case I mean that literally) and then say, "God, where were you?" Well, the truth is He has never left us. We are the ones who have turned our backs on God and wandered down our own wayward trail.

DISCUSSION

- *Was Scott planning to meet his future wife that day?*
- *Does God laugh?*
- *Have you ever asked God, "What is your plan?"*

Proposal

THIS IS WHAT I WROTE in my journal on April 19, 2007:

What a day. Got up at 5:00 after being up until 3:00. Went out and ran some appointments. Came home. Debbie went out on the patio to read the Bible. I was exhausted and lay down for two minutes and slept. I woke with a crystal-clear vision, a message from the Holy Spirit. That still, small, quiet voice in your head that provides guidance and comfort, direction, and discipline. The Holy Spirit will never lie to you. He always wants the best for you. That quiet voice told me to propose and marry Debbie, and that God would bless the union.

So I went out on the patio and sat with Debbie; I kept looking up to Heaven, communicating with God that I love her. A conversation with God that probably took only a few seconds seemed like hours, but finally I decided, okay, I'll do it. I kissed her hand and asked her to marry me. Of course, she said yes because, unbeknownst to me, she had been having a similar internal conversation and fully believed that this was God's will. She was very worried about what her family would say. I pointed out that I wasn't marrying her family. I was marrying Debbie, and I promised to show my love for her for the rest of our lives. We immediately told my mother. She thought we were joking. After a long silence, she looked at me and said, "Congratulations." She then turned to Debbie and said, "I'm sorry." But I said, no, we were serious. We really are getting married. After phoning her family and giving them the news, we left for the nearby shopping mall to purchase an engagement ring.

Proposal

After ring shopping, we decided to celebrate at my favorite eating place, Henry's Diner. Of course, I showed off my bride-to-be and a new engagement ring. I am a natural showman and a flash git (as they say in England). Everyone at Henry's was happy for us, and we felt so fearfully and wonderfully made, and now we were "promised" together.

DISCUSSION

- *Can God use tragedy for good results?*
- *Can God use our bad choices for the fulfillment of his plan?*
- *Is tragedy part of God's plan?*

England

ALTHOUGH I HAVE BEEN TO Mexico and the Bahamas, this was my first trip out of the North American continent. I traveled over there to meet my future in-laws and mainly to see my wife to be. It was a great success overall. I distributed over 250 books one by one in twelve days. I met some good people, some not so good. God loves them, so I love them. I spoke at a church. It went very well. I invited her parents, and they came.

Part of the reason I hated the trip was because on the plane going over I felt the worst pain I can ever remember in my right shoulder. Coming home from England I was very sick on the plane.

The main reason I even went to England was to see Debbie.

I got home and at midnight the next day went and taped three TV shows. Then I went to my best friend's house and saw him, his wife, and his son right after he got off work.

Overall, it was a good trip. But I really didn't like England. They drive on the wrong side of the road (literally). I couldn't drive over there, and I felt like a caged rat. It sucks being totally dependant again on other people to go anywhere. I didn't know anything over there or where it was. Before I came home I knew where McDonald's was.

DISCUSSION

Scott is self-reliant; he does not like being dependent.

- *What part did this attribute play in his accident?*
- *Can he change?*
- *How does God encourage him to change?*
- *How does God encourage you to change?*

Emotional Ramblings

I AM VERY PROUD OF several things that were happening after my wreck. Lost souls were always coming to the Kingdom. That's what life is all about right now. We all have different lives and journeys. God is in control of all of us who follow Him. God gives everyone their own choice. You play, you pay.

When I was very sad and depressed, I prayed for an orange-and-white cat, and a neighbor brought me an orange-and-white cat, who was doing nothing but meowing all the time. I prayed over the cat, and he calmed down. He is the best cat we have now, and we have about fifteen of them. Most of them are wild. I was so sad—my best friend was a cat.

In December of 2006 my best friend, Doug Holiday, was diagnosed with a brain tumor. I know what it feels like to lie in a hospital bed, and I know what it feels like to anticipate surgery, the fear of the pain, the dread of rehabilitation. But I have no idea how a brain tumor feels. But God knows, and God cares. Doug's surgery went well, and he's getting better every day. One thing I do know; after surgery it can take quite a while to heal and sometimes even longer to "feel" well again. The keys to a successful rehabilitation are patience, persistence, and a forward outlook.

Debbie and I go distributing books in the Old Market, Omaha, Nebraska, a lot. One day we met a guy in the Old Market, where I was passing out books. He was a nice man who rode motorcycles and had Harley Davidson tattoos. He told me that my name and story were mentioned at an AA meeting he attended in Colorado about a month and a half before. He piped up and said, "Hey, I know that guy!" And some other people there also knew me. This was before the concept of "viral marketing" became commonplace. It was just one guy telling the next. Nevertheless, my story continues to get out there, and now, with the advent of today's information-based technology, my story can travel faster, farther, and reach more people. God is preparing for a major explosion onto the world scene. If He selects my story as part of His message, I pray I remain humble and give all the glory where it goes, to God.

Dreams and Visions

THIS IS WHAT HAPPENED TO me one night when God told me to get out of bed and write. I didn't, and I couldn't go back to sleep, so I got up and wrote. God said, "You can do nothing without me; I am everything; don't put your trust in things of this world"—that includes everyone.

I didn't listen to the Holy Spirit, and I couldn't go to sleep until I did listen to the Holy Spirit.

We all need to step out of our comfort zones and expand our horizons. I was a sports jock, but I never played or tried hockey. A friend and his wife and Debbie and I went to a hockey game, and I loved it. Now I realize I was wrong living with an "I like this sport or I don't like that sport" attitude. You need to step out of your own comfort zones and experience what God has to offer you—even if it is not the sort of thing you think you would like. No one can force you to do anything. If you want to remain in your old humdrum life, don't whine to me.

Technology is getting too smart for its own good. Technology is doubling every two years now. Like the old TV shows, *The Jetsons* and *Star Trek*, warp speed here we come. The world will be like *The Jetsons* before it is all over. We need to realize as long as we give God all the praise He deserves we'll be all right. If not, calamity will result. This old boy says, "There will be no wine before it's time." We cannot make God do anything, He is the Great Physician. He has a master plan. If we all think we're so smart, God laughs at us. After all I've been through, beyond a shadow of a doubt God is the supreme being. We are all dots in God's master plan. We think we are so important, me included. But God knows what we are going to do before we even do it. What a God we serve!

Do not think you are alone. We all freak out, me included. Try this one on for size. Do you want to walk a mile in my shoes? Coma nine months, fourteen surgeries, didn't get married until my thirty-ninth birthday. Yes, I was wondering "What is going on?" God has a master plan. I am so happy now I can't stand myself. Good thing my wife can. My wife says I'm a good bloke. Bottom line—that is my number one concern on earth, pleasing her. I know, I know, I know she loves me.

Coming back from a meeting, it hit me that I am an example for the world. It made me freak out, but the only comforting thing was I know who is in control, and He will never give me more than I can handle. Whenever I get to the point where things are going really well for me and I think I am all of that and then some, God gives me another dose of humble pie and humbles me. That is a good thing. God hates pride. My cockiness is in the Lord, and there isn't anything wrong with that. God wants us to rely on Him.

At the time of writing this, I am feeling pretty good right now after having taken a couple of weeks off from writing. It is good to rest sometimes.

We need to prioritize what is going on in our lives right now. The Holy Spirit told me, *Whoa!* What do people care about what is going on in your life? We all have a God-given plan and purpose for our lives.

I can't force people—will not even try—neither will God.

I just want to tell people how great God is and how much He will do for you if you call upon the Name of Jesus Christ.

I'm really feeling kind of overwhelmed with all I want to accomplish in this world in my life. But I have to remember I can accomplish nothing by myself. I think I'll let God worry about it.

God has all the hairs on our heads numbered. I want to challenge anyone who knows the number of hairs on everyone's heads to call me and let me know; I will personally be their servant for life.

I do feel a bit guilty. I have way too much fun wherever I go in life. An example would be going out to eat with my friends, laughing, choking on my food, and little kids looking at me with their mouths open. This happened at a McDonalds in Lake Manawa where I was meeting a good friend called Joe. We call him Yo Joe. We laugh and have a good time wherever we go. The thing is true with whomever I'm with; we have a good time. I'm a bit of a joker and show off everywhere I go. Someone has to do it. I'll take that call. Many, many people will attest to that. It is one of my many faults.

Of course, I have problems; who doesn't? But I don't *really* have any problems—neither do any of you. Give everything to God. He has shoulders big enough to carry any problem. You have to remember we were not created to handle any problems. God is God. We all think we're important or special, and we are to God. One thing I insist on, whatever the situation, is laughing and having a good time. Life is too short to get bent out of shape over a small problem. I have noticed this wherever I go. People freak out over things not really important. Just deal with it and get on down the road.

In the Old Market in Omaha, Nebraska, it was 90 degrees outside. I was dripping sweat, and an old woman came up to me and gave me a cold bottle of water. She said, "You look like you need this." It touched me that some people really do appreciate and care what I am trying to accomplish. Some people don't care whether I live or die, and that's okay. The number one reason I work myself so hard is because I care about other people and lost souls more than I care about myself.

I have a lot more problems than most people, but I do work harder than most to try to improve myself every day. An old quote from my old sports background keeps coming to my mind. The quote is from Vince Lombardi: "Winning isn't everything; it's the only thing." I will not accept failure in anything I do, and neither should you. Jesus says in 1 Corinthians 9:24–26: "Do you not know that in a race all the runners run, but only one gets the prize? Run in such a way as to get the prize. Everyone who competes in the games goes into strict training. They do it to get a crown that will not last; but we do it to get a crown that will last forever. Therefore I do not run like a man running aimlessly; I do not fight like a man beating the air."

There is one thing that is an answer to any problem anyone has—the answer is always God. Father knows best.

DISCUSSION

- Has Scott changed since his accident?
- How?
- Is there still some of the "old Scott" left?
- Can you think of examples of the old versus new Scott?

My Friend

TOM COMES OUT TO MY house every Tuesday night at 7:00, and we have a great time together.

When I first met Tom, he was working security at a Louis Palau concert in Omaha, Nebraska. At the end of the concert, I tried to get on the stage, but I will be truthful: I was trying to get on the stage the whole concert. I wanted to tell everyone about God and what He has done for me. Tom was trying to decide, "Is this guy a nut ball, or is he for real?" He escorted me out through the crowd after the program, and it took me forty-five minutes to go two blocks, and everyone was saying, "Hi, Scott" and hugging me. Tom decided I was for real and has been helping me ever since.

We talked for quite a while after the program, which led to us meeting every week.

Tom arranged a speaking engagement for me at the Omaha chapter of the Christian Motorcyclists Association. It went very well; I think the people appreciate the honesty I show in the presentation. Only God knows.

I speak very regularly at the Open Door Mission in Omaha, Nebraska. Don't get paid for it; it is my way of trying to give back to the community and help people.

A Letter from Stephanie

HI, SCOTT!
You probably don't remember me, but I met you down in the Heartland of America Park with my husband and kids a couple of weeks ago. I have to say, it was a real pleasure to meet you, and I really do believe that I was meant to run into you that day. Even before I met you, I was thinking to myself, "Why are we walking all the way down here to have a picnic?" My husband was even trying to convince me that we should just eat lunch near the Old Market, but I kept insisting that we go down and be near the water fountain. I didn't know why I was so persistent until I met you. You know, I am not an avid church participant, but *I do* believe in God, and *I do believe in fate*, and I know I was supposed to meet you that day.

After our talk and when we went our separate ways, I went home and read your book. I thought about it for a long time and thought about your life experiences and all that you'd been through. You and your book have really made an impact on me. The same day that I finished your book, I spoke with my brother who lives in Houston. He was just like you when he was younger. He was good looking, popular, athletic, and quite the charmer. But now he is thirty-eight years old and addicted to cocaine. I am extremely close to my brother, and it kills me to see him throw his life away. Unfortunately, I'm all too familiar with addictions. I am the youngest of eight kids, and out of all of us, only three remaining have never had any kind of drug or alcohol addiction. Luckily, I am one of those three. So, because I have been through this several times, I know not to enable him, but I don't know how to help him, especially from so far away! He is pretty far gone and on several occasions, I have feared that he would kill himself or somebody else.

In fact, one time he called me and said he was going to blow his brains out but that the bullet was in the wrong barrel. That same night he called again, and, while on the phone with me, he almost got in a car accident. I yelled at him and told him to put the gun to his head and make sure the bullet was in the right barrel this time and to do himself in before he kills someone and then I hung up on him.

Tim was very successful and had a great paying job and ownership with a business in Texas. I was so proud of all he had accomplished. Then, as my dad was dying of cancer, is when it all came crashing down. He really got worse; his supervisors were sick of his behavior; they fired him and bought out his portion of the ownership, paying him a large amount of money. He spent it all on drugs in an instant. He now lives in his house (not for long) with no water, electricity, or food. He is at an extreme low point in his life and, like you, has had several warnings from God to stop. One of these days, he will run out of those warnings.

The day that I met you, I called him. I told him about our meeting downtown and how speaking with you and running into you that day was not an "accident." Our meeting was meant to be, and spreading your message to my brother was also meant to be. My brother was speechless and broke down and cried. I sent him your book just a couple of days ago, and if I ever get him back to Omaha, I would like him to meet you. I'm sure you have been told this before, but you are a very "effective" person. Not just because of what happened to you but how you have dealt with it; that's what is so remarkable. I know you have been through horrible times and still struggle today, but I am inspired by the way you took a tragic situation and have made something positive come from it. Whether you know it or not, you are helping others past and present. I was telling my best friend about you during our conversation at the park, and she said she had met you once a while back. She, too, was touched by your story and agreed that your experiences could help my brother.

I think you are an extraordinary person, and I feel very lucky to have met you!!

> Take care of yourself!!!
> *Stephanie*

Cheryl

IT WAS AN ORDINARY DAY, or so I thought. I had just finished taking a class on medical billing through the U.S. Career Institute. One of my ideas was doing a home-based business. I had finished the class and was out looking for prospects so I could work at home. I had the confidence that finally I had found what I had been looking for since the year 2000.

I said it was an ordinary day, but it wasn't. It was different. I didn't quite know what it was, but it was different. I was going to a lot of places, looking for prospects, and really didn't know which way to turn at times. But somehow I kept turning the right way. Then I got hungry and decided to take a break from my prospecting. It was going to be a short break—and then back to work. But I couldn't decide whether I wanted Burger King or McDonalds. Then the decision was made without me even realizing it. It was as though someone or something was guiding me all day. I just knew it had to be God leading me, so I felt good and confident that this new-found possible home business was going to work. But instead he was leading me to something else. Something much better and more powerful. I turned in McDonald's parking lot and went in to eat. When I got in there, I saw someone I used to talk to in college. I couldn't remember his name, but I knew him as an acquaintance. I say this because he would stop me and talk to me in the hallways at Iowa Western, but I never knew him. He had told me about his car wreck back then somewhat, but I never really knew what all happened.

At that time in my life I simply didn't care about much of what was going on with anybody else because I was too wrapped up in my own pains of life. And I was about as far away from God as you could get. In fact, at that time in my life I thought He was my enemy. I thought He was the one causing all my grief. I didn't realize that it was Satan doing all this in my life.

Anyway, to shorten my story a bit, when I entered McDonalds, I saw Scott McPhillips and his girlfriend at the time. I debated whether to say hi or pretend I didn't see Scott. Not because of him but because I kind of wanted to just slip in and eat real quick and then get back out prospecting. But I saw his girlfriend, Debbie, holding some bottles of Juice Plus. This was one of my ventures trying home businesses, so I decided to say hi to them. I did not know what I was in for. "Hi" turned into "Would you like to join us for lunch?" How could I say no? That would have been very rude. So, while I was standing in line at McDonalds, Scott handed me his card. I thought to myself, "Oh, no, he is going to try to sell me Juice Plus." To my amazement it was no ordinary card he handed me. It was about his car wreck and how he had accidentally killed someone because he was high and drunk. *Wow!!!* Now I knew this was not an ordinary day. I had never ever read a card like that one before. It was powerful. It was like my life just changed with reading that card. I felt a power over me saying, "Okay, Cheryl, I have been trying to reach you, and I keep getting disconnected. This time you are going to listen." So I sat down with Scott and Debbie, and Scott told me he had written a book. He didn't tell me that he was, in fact, trying to sell me something, but it was something no one had ever been able to sell me before.

My curiosity got the best of me, and I bought both books: *Superman* and *Superman II*. I was in a hurry to get home to see just what I had bought. I had wondered what exactly happened to Scott, but now I was about to read it for myself. I did not know that this was God's plan to save me from my ruins. I thought everything was going well. But here in these books I learned more than ever before about God. My mom had tried to reach me with God to no avail. Others had tried to no avail. I carried around great anger inside me for years, crying to God for help but then cursing him the next minute. I did not think God was on my side at all.

After reading both of Scott's books, which I had a hard time putting down—and even on my way home from McDonalds that day—I knew something was different. Scott had asked me at McDonalds to pray with him and Debbie. I had never prayed in public like this before, but I agreed, and I did. That was the most powerful prayer I ever felt. It changed my life. Although I had always believed in God, I was not living His will. Now I do. I am not saying I don't make mistakes because I do. I am human, after all. But that day with Scott and Debbie changed my life because through talking to them and reading his books I came to know God. I always believed He existed but never really knew Him. Now, thanks to Scott and Debbie, I know God. He is my father and even more God is the best friend I could ever have. And He can be your best friend too. All you have to do is read these books or even better pick up a Bible and read it. All the answers to any question you may have in life are right there. You just have to read it and believe it and your life will be forever changed.

There are two paths in life. God's path and Satan's path. Which path will you choose? I hope God's path because Satan's path is a dead end and leads to nowhere but self-destruction. So, open your heart and let God in before it is too late. None of us knows how long we are on this Earth for or when the world will end. So don't you want to be ready when the end of the world comes? I know I do. I know where I am going, and it is much better than this place they call Earth. How do I know where I am going? Because I accepted the Lord Jesus Christ in my life, and I am letting Him call the shots now, not me anymore. If you continue down this path you call "my life," you get exactly a mess you call "my life." But if you let Jesus Christ in your life and let Him lead you the way to righteousness, you can finally be at peace and live a good, happy, peaceful life. Just hand it over to Him, and He will take care of everything.

Anyway, enough of my ministry. This book is about Scott McPhillips's story, not mine. So I will end by saying I am happy to say Scott and Debbie got married and I attended the wedding. I also go to church with Scott and Debbie now. It is a church that truly believes in God, not in religion. To learn more, you will have to read Scott's books *Superman* and *Superman II*. He talks of this church in the second book. When I read about this church, I knew I had to go there. I think I have been going there for probably over a year now, and it has changed my life. I used to read the Bible but didn't understand it; now, I understand it. I understand it because I let Jesus Christ into my life, and He helps me to understand what it is all about through my new-found friends at church, Scott and Debbie and F. C. Farwell and his family. But the person who leads our church—or should I say the people who lead our church—have taught me how to understand the Bible so that now I live with the word of God in me. And it is *wonderful!!!* Thank you, Scott and Debbie McPhillips and those others who have led me to God and even more have become my brothers and sisters in Christ.

Jesus and God are the answer to any question you may have in life. Just open that book they call the Bible and let it speak to you. It has a lot to tell you. After all, it is the basic instructions before leaving Earth. Bet you didn't know that and neither did I until someone told me. Good luck with your life, and I pray that you make the right decision in your life and follow the Lord Jesus Christ before it is too late. Because no one knows when the Lord Jesus Christ is coming back, but He is coming back. I can't wait for that day. I am ready. Are you?

Lauri

IT IS NOT EVERY DAY that a customer—a complete stranger—comes up to you out of the blue and asks, "Are you a Christian?" When something like that happens, you realize God is involved, so you tend to pay attention!!

In April of 2008 that's exactly what happened in the shop I work at in Old Town here in Kissimmee, Florida. When I said, yes, this twenty-ish-year-old man handed me two books, explaining that since he was Jewish, he thought someone else might get more out of them than he would. He said he had just bought them from this thirty-nine-year-old man walking (rather awkwardly) around Old Town, talking to people about his story and selling his books. He sheepishly stated he bought them because he felt *so* sorry for him—he looked as though he had been in a train wreck.

I knew God had placed this special man, Scott McPhillips, in my path for a reason, so, since it was a slow night, I began thumbing through the first book. I finished both that very night. After some phone calls the next day, I was able to meet up with him and his new pretty English wife, Debbie, at a nearby hotel as they periodically come here from their home in Iowa to spread Scott's story and ministry. I have considered them precious friends ever since.

Scott's story is a jaw-dropping, simply *amazing* one of hope, redemption, and inspiration. Hopefully, perhaps, Scott's story will bless and inspire you to pass on his message as it did me.

DISCUSSION
- *Would you consider Scott to be a bold individual?*
- *In what ways?*
- *Is boldness a good trait?*
- *How does God use Scott's boldness?*
- *How does Satan use Scott's boldness?*

Joe

WHEN I FIRST MET SCOTT about ten years ago, it was at an Overcomers in Christ meeting. I wasn't quite sure how to take him; Scott's approach to ministry was a little unorthodox to me as he was kind of loud and difficult to understand. As the months and years have gone by, I've come to know Scott as a man who loves the Lord and that God uses us all in different ways. I have seen God use Scott in ways that He could never use anyone else, largely because of his testimony. He has been very consistent with God's calling in his life, sharing the love of Jesus through his books, personality, and determination to draw others to our Savior. Scott has never allowed his physical limitations and pain to slow him down in his efforts to share the gospel wherever he goes.

Recently, Scott's life has changed dramatically. He met the love of his life, Debbie, married her, and has become the father of a beautiful baby girl, Rose. I have seen him grow into a loving husband and gentle father who has truly touched my heart. This is a different Scott than the man I met ten years ago—but with the same drive and determination. With Debbie and Rose by his side, I know God will continue to use this family in mighty ways to further His Kingdom. I'm looking forward to seeing how God will use this precious family in the coming years. We don't know what the future holds, but we know who holds the future!!!

In Christ's Love,
Joseph Skinner

"I can do all things through Christ who strengthens me."
—Philippians 4:13

Gaylord Schelling

SCOTT HAS CHANGED A GREAT deal since his accident. His growth as a Christian has been phenomenal, as he has developed into a person who is not afraid to speak to people openly about his relationship with God. He publicly seeks people to share the good news. Whether it is through his published books, social networking, or speaking engagements, Scott wants to lead others to an understanding of what Christ can do for them.

Scott has memorized many scriptures that speak to him on a personal level. His phone greeting is "Praise the Lord! This is Scott. How can I help you?" This truly shows the change in Scott from his high school and college days where the Lord was not a part of his life. This new relationship with God has made Scott a better person.

After Scott married Deb, he has gone through even greater changes as a man. Deb has brought a sense of calmness and further direction to Scott. Although Scott has always been very independent, he has learned through his marriage that he can allow himself to be both an independent thinker but also dependent on someone else for emotional and spiritual growth. Scott has embraced marriage and has earned the love and respect of a wonderful young woman. Deb is a quiet young woman, but she has learned to assert herself with Scott. It is amazing to watch Scott listen to Deb, evaluate his own personal thoughts, and to then accept and respect Deb for her uniqueness and her beliefs. She has been instrumental in bringing Scott to even stronger Christian beliefs.

Scott and Deb have a strong Christian marriage filled with mutual love and trust. Where one is weak, the other is strong. They truly have a relationship where each one gives and takes to make the marriage work. They spend a great deal of time together because Scott cannot work full-time because of his injuries. Many marriages would struggle with so much time together. Scott and Deb complement each other and are great parents to their child. At one time, Scott thought he would never know the joys of parenthood. The role of father to baby Rose has made him even stronger and more determined to be a role model to others. Rose is loved and treasured by both Scott and Deb. When Scott holds Rose, he is truly content with life.

Scott's mother Beverly has been a strong support for Scott's struggles after the accident. She continues to be there for both Scott and Deb. She does not hover but instead gives them the support when necessary but allows them to make their own successes and failures in life. With Beverly's example, Scott and Deb have become a strong, independent family unit.

God has a purpose in life for Scott, Deb, and Rose. Some people would have become bitter and would have given up after a life-altering accident. Scott never quit fighting and worked to achieve the highest level of independence possible after an accident that would have caused most people to give up. As Scott continues to grow in Christian faith, he will be setting an example not only for the young people who hear him speak but also for his daughter Rose. May God continue to richly bless this family!

Gaylord Schelling

A Precarious Balance

ONCE AGAIN, AS IS MY pattern, tonight I received a sobering reminder of the delicateness of my physical ability while enjoying a raucous conversation with a friend. As he neared the doorway to leave, we traded sarcastic verbal jabs and were near hysterics. As my body heaved with laughter, suddenly I lost my balance and toppled backward. Hitting the carpet flat on my back, I felt my head slam against the floor. Everything in sight became an immediate blur, except for the twinkling of stars. Praise be to God, though, I had not landed on anything—no furniture and not on a tiled floor. Nothing broke (including me). I am still a little lightheaded as I write this, some two hours after I fell. Over the years since my accident, I no longer feel it necessary to take pills to mask the pain; not that the pain is less, but I've gotten better at managing it. But, admittedly, I did take two pills tonight. I need to become more mindful of the tenuous and delicate balance I navigate between walking upright and being an invalid or worse. Every so often, God sends me that reminder. Sometimes it really hurts. I am not ready to be totally dependent on Debbie, and I certainly am not ready to leave her behind. As my mother will testify, it can be very taxing managing me; the struggle is not just mine to endure. But at least for now, I'm lying comfortably on the couch with my wife. My head is a little fuzzy, yet even now Debbie is one beautiful soul.

Highs and Lows

I'VE TRAVELED MANY HILLS AND valleys throughout life. The key to a victorious life, in my opinion, is not to get too high or too low. Maintain a balance, a constant rhythm. It's natural for my personality to soar like a rocket during the great times and then sink into a God-questioning depression during the low times. One thing always remains the same. God is always there, no matter what. He patiently waits for my spirit to brighten, as I regularly fail to live up to my vision of what I think God expects of me. Yet God never fails. And I thank him daily that he does not give me what I deserve.

DISCUSSION

- *Does God always give us what we ask for?*
- *Does God always give us what we deserve?*
- *Are there earthly consequences for our actions?*
- *Are there heavenly implications for our actions?*

Healing

TODAY DANIEL, WHOM DEBBIE AND I had met at the Cox Cable network some months ago, called us unexpectedly. A devout Christian man, he told us he had felt the Holy Spirit prompting him to call us. He was in the midst of arranging a conference for Pastor Leo Strathman and his assistant, Donna. As we attended Pastor Strathman's conference, via Daniel's invitation, we became very good friends with Daniel and his wife, Victoria, and Pastor Leo and Donna. We faithfully attended every session and have benefited greatly from the pastor's knowledge and from his friendship.

Among many topics presented, there was a focus on the literal, physical healing of God. Of course, I could use some healing! At one point during the first meeting with Pastor Strathman, I watched in awe as my left leg grew as he prayed for me. It was totally cool.

I told everyone I knew about my experience at the first meeting, yet only one friend made the effort to come to the next meeting. I think he was hungry for more of God. At the following meeting he brought his mother, who had been healed as a direct result of what had transpired at the conference.

So what happened to my other friends? I think it is difficult for most people to seek after God with their whole heart, soul, and mind. Well, I can't force anyone to believe, whether in reference to the healing of their body or, for that matter, their spirit. I admit that sometimes I try to force God's hand, like I want to reap the harvest when I am simply the guy who plants the seeds. I often feel convicted of this when I talk with Jesus.

As the conference progressed, one day Debbie and I went out for lunch with Pastor Leo and Donna. We were eating with them at a restaurant in Omaha where we were talking, laughing, and praising Jesus. Our enthusiasm was unbounded; I was so excited at what I had witnessed at the conference. My fervor got the best of me when I suddenly yelled, "Jesus!" I was praising; I did not mean to disrespect my Savior. But the manager immediately came over to our table and asked us to leave right away. The manager told us, "Don't worry about the bill—we'll cover it, but you have to leave right now." So we were kicked out because I yelled, "Jesus!"

Thank you, Jesus. I am sorry if people were offended, but it is interesting that when Christians become too enthusiastic, we are out of place and people feel very uncomfortable—uncomfortable with the truth, at least when it is openly displayed.

Looking back at it, the situation ended in victory for Jesus. And as an added benefit we all had a free meal and a good laugh. Some may have wanted us to feel humiliated and embarrassed, but we had the victory in Christ.

DISCUSSION

- *In what ways would Scott be a difficult friend?*
- *How is Scott always "balancing" his life?*
- *In what ways do you balance your own life?*
- *How do you know when your life is out of balance?*

Orlando, 2009

DEBBIE AND I DROVE TO Orlando, Florida, for my forty-first birthday and our second anniversary. It is a long drive but worth it. We went five hundred miles a day for three days going down and 750 miles a day for two days coming home. That's a hard trip for anybody, but for a body like mine it is pure torture.

The first week we stayed at Vacation Villas at Fantasy World, the resort where we first met. Romance was in the air. We met a lot of British people during the first week of the holiday, which was an added bonus for Debbie. I share her soft spot toward the Brits, thanks to my wonderful wife.

The second week we stayed at Florida Vacation Villas. My mother had stayed there the previous year. The first night we were there, we met Don and Diane. Of course, they remembered me from last year when I had visited my mother. (I'd given them one of my books.) Don asked whether we were going to any of the parks. We said, "Oh, no, they are too expensive." He said, "Would you go if you could go for free?" Of course we said, "Yes." He said, "I can get you in for free; we'll go to whatever Disney park you want." He told us he had worked there for eighteen years. We went to Animal Kingdom on Monday, November 9th, my birthday and our anniversary.

The Safari jeep driver in the park, a jovial African American woman, told us we got a real birthday and anniversary treat because all the animals, zebras, giraffes, elephants, and rhinos were coming right up to the jeep. The lady driver said she had never seen this many animals come this close to the jeep in one trip. It was a real gift from God Almighty.

Our day at Animal Kingdom was an overwhelming success. We were there for over six hours, then returned to our villa and slept very well. That sort of physical and mental stimulation can really wear me out. We had such a memorable time. Disney World is a great place for kids of all ages; it's one of those places that everyone needs to go sometime in their lives.

Don and Diane were absolutely selfless in their care of Debbie and me during our time in Florida. I really did feel bad, as Don, a sixty-eight-year-old man, pushed me through the park, hills, and all in a wheelchair. But I really could not walk because of my knees. By the end of the day everyone with me wished I had a motorized wheelchair; I wore them out! I am not light at 205 lbs. I guess I should really work on losing fifteen or twenty more pounds because the extra weight causes pain in my left knee when I walk. But, on the other hand, that wheelchair is nice, especially when I get to jump the queue everywhere I go, including airports and amusement parks. I do tend to get special treatment when I am in a wheelchair. Do I agree with that? Wholeheartedly! We spent two days with Don and Diane.

We also met a very nice man at Florida Vacation Villas named Paul. While I was resting in our room, my wife met him in the pool. They had struck up a conversation; Paul is easy to talk to and a great storyteller. The conversation worked its way to me and the fact that I was writing books and using my broken body for Christ's witness. Paul actually accompanied Debbie to our room, where I met him and sold him a couple books. I meet so many people, and as is most often the case, I assume I'll probably never see them again on this Earth.

But the next day Paul returned and bought more books. And the next day he came back again and got even more! We discovered he is a retired Lutheran pastor, and he was giving them to all his friends and associates. Once again, Christ just drops an opportunity in my lap to witness for His glory. Paul has even begun to line up some opportunities for me to return to Florida and speak to a couple church groups. As always, I guess I'll just wait on God and see what happens!

DISCUSSION

Scott lives a life on "borrowed time."

- *In what ways does this concept apply to everyone?*
- *In what ways are we to be good stewards of what God has given us?*
- *How has Scott made the most of what he has been given?*
- *How can we best serve God's purpose?*

Summary

SCOTT MCPHILLIPS CHANGES LIVES JUST by his living. Lying beneath his bent and broken exterior is a complex personality. His external persona is dynamic, hard-driven, and jovial. But just beneath his "changed" personality, his humanness still lingers; spend a little time with Scott, and it is easy to see that he fights his failures each and every day. He can be moody and brooding, particularly when he is tired. His body often wears down and is the governor of his outreach, but the marathon of Scott's life is broken into an unending series of daily sprints that tax his physical, mental, and spiritual stamina to its maximum.

Just mention his wife, Debbie, in conversation, and Scott's countenance immediately changes from a cocky, crowing rooster into a sentimental and loving little puppy. Scott knows that he is blessed indeed, for God has matched him with a soul mate for eternity despite his history of using and sometimes abusing women throughout his athletic career. Debbie is an undeserved gift.

Scott prides himself in his never-give-up approach to life. And pride is so ingrained in him that I sometimes get the impression that Scott is "proud of not being proud." I often think that he must burn through friends quicker than most people because Scott is high-output and high-maintenance, both physically and socially.

But get through all the bravado, pride, and cockiness, and there stands Scott—a big-hearted, broken, and triumphant warrior. Every day alive is a victorious miracle; no day arrives without Scott's constant companion: pain. Pain so deep that it cripples him, slurs his speech, and clouds his judgment. Pain so evident that his knees swell like watermelons, his shoulders send aches up into his neck, and his hands remain in a permanent, disfigured curl. He takes pain medication just to make it through the waking hours, and when he has taken too much his speech and thought patterns become slow, snarled, and scattered. Scott has confronted this demon every single day since his fateful one in October of 1989. Yet Scott smiles throughout it all, as is his special gift.

Scott has a message for the world, a message he loves to shout at the top of his lungs. The irony is that he really does not have to shout at all; all he has to do is simply and humbly tell his story of bad attitudes, terrible choices, and God's endless grace. The listener is thereby confronted face-to-face with the endless love of Christ, who must be saving one amazing body for Scott's eternity with Him. It is Scott's presence that does the talking; it is his daily struggle to live that conveys God's message of love and grace to the world.

Epilogue

THE DAYS WERE BEGINNING TO feel action-packed, just the way I like it. I could see that this was going to be coming along soon. We're headed to Branson, Missouri, for a week of street evangelism and book sales, which always seems to create a whirlwind atmosphere of trying to think on your feet. On the other hand, it will be good to get away from the city pace of Omaha for a while, even if I'm only trading one chaotic schedule for another. And while I'm there, I'll see an old friend, Leroy New, whom I know because the first time my mother and I went to Branson, we saw his show and talked to him afterward, and we really hit it off. Every time we go to Branson now, we always visit him. He has a very good show everyone should see when they go to Branson or the surrounding area. What I really do like about him is he is a real pastor. He lets me speak for a few minutes every time I am at his Church service on Sunday mornings.

Things are really going quite well for Deb and me these days. We work so hard for God sometimes, but I believe that God rewards us for our efforts. Our unborn child is getting closer to his "world entry" every day. I know that things will be turned upside down once the baby arrives. Just like our baby, I think I'll have some growing to do too; some people tell me it will be time for me to grow up. Life will no longer be about me or Debbie and me; it will be all about the needs of that little baby. I'm ready for the change in focus. It is what I have been praying for, that little "flesh of my flesh" gift from God.

Michael Raymond McPhillips: Mommy and daddy love you very much and cannot wait for your arrival. Our excitement grows daily more and more.

And then...

On September 23, 2010, at 12:05 P.M. CST Rose Ann McPhillips made her entry into the world! What a gift. That's all I could say. What a gift! We love her to death. Okay, so I thought the baby would be a boy, but my happiness in Baby Rose goes beyond words. People stop by the house often with gifts for little Rose. I can see already that there are plenty of people quite willing to spoil her. Even my in-laws in England are growing closer since Rose's birth.

God is absolutely blowing me away. I've come into contact with no fewer than ten people in the last two weeks who have given their lives to Christ. God moves in unsearchable ways; I can see a revival of hearts coming soon. Even as Debbie and I know that we are God's people, little baby Rose is all-encompassing right now. It is amazing how that bundle of joy can occupy so much of my focus, even though she doesn't do much right now except eat, sleep, and poop. There are times when I think that doesn't sound like such a bad life. I am anticipating the stages to come and what Rose will be doing in the days, weeks, and months down the road from now.

Even in the midst of Rose's birth, God was at work throughout the hospital. Rose was 20 inches long and weighed 7 lbs., 11 oz. at birth. I stayed in the hospital overnight with Deb and the baby, and three nurses came to accept Christ that night in the hospital: one male nurse and two female nurses. One of the Christ-conversions happened around 4 A.M.! This is a very special reunion for me to spend this time at Creighton Hospital in Omaha. Here I am today, watching the birth of my daughter and watching God bring nurses unto Himself. Twenty-one years ago (it was called St Joseph's Hospital back then), I was life-flighted here after my accident. God has brought my life full-circle since then.

Now that Rose has arrived and we have brought her home, life is easing back into our normally hectic routine, including introducing people to the Kingdom and walking them to life in Christ. To me, this is normal life.

I take my role of father and husband very seriously, and I wish that this was the norm. Sadly, in many homes fathers are absent or disengaged, and they do not heed the call of God in their lives. It seems they often only serve themselves, despite their responsibilities as a husband and father. This world so desperately needs an outpouring of the Holy Spirit, a boldness in the lives of Christian believers. Yes, my life is changing with sweet

Epilogue

baby Rose, but I'll never stop serving God. And I'll never stop telling the story of how this self-centered party boy paid an awful price for his sinful lifestyle and yet God cared enough to send his son, Jesus Christ, to pay the heavenly price for my wicked choices even as I paid the earthly price. This is my life. This is Scott McPhillips.

Give the gift of inspiration!

— ORDER HERE —

Please send me:

_____ copies of *Superman Doesn't Live Here Anymore I*

_____ copies of *Superman Doesn't Live Here Anymore II*

_____ copies of *Superman Doesn't Live Here Anymore III*

TOTAL AMOUNT

Each book is $10.00 <u>OR</u> get 3 books for $28.00 .... _____

*Please add $3.00 shipping per book .... _____

*Iowa residents please add $.60 tax per book .... _____

TOTAL ENCLOSED............................... _____

Allow 15 days for delivery.
(Canadian orders must be accompanied by a postal money order in U.S. funds.)

❏ **YES**, I am interested in having Scott McPhillips speak or give a seminar to my company, association, school, or organization. Please send information.

Name _____

Organization _____

Address _____

City/State/Zip _____

Phone _____ Email _____

Please make your check payable and return to:
Mac on the Attack for Jesus
28535 Coldwater Ave. • Honey Creek, Iowa 51542

Call your order to: (712) 545-4477 or (712) 309-5850
Web site: **hey-scott.com**   Email: scott.mcphillips@yahoo.com

AD Non Fiction
813 D481s

Dethlefsen, Bruce, 1948 – Something near the
dance floor   9000996771

DISCARDED BY THE
MEAD PUBLIC LIBRARY
SHEBOYGAN, WI

9000996771